Oxford Read and Di

T0050546

Farms

Rachel Bladon

Contents

OXFORD
UNIVERSITY PRESS

OXFORD

UNIVERSITY PRESS

Great Clarendon Street, Oxford, OX2 6DP, United Kingdom

Oxford University Press is a department of the University
of Oxford. It furthers the University's objective of excellence in
research, scholarship, and education by publishing worldwide.
Oxford is a registered trade mark of Oxford University Press
in the UK and in certain other countries

© Oxford University Press 2012

The moral rights of the author have been asserted

First published in 2012

2016 2015 2014 2013 2012

10 9 8 7 6 5 4 3 2 1

ISBN: 978 0 19 464683 3

An Audio CD Pack containing this book and a CD is also
available, ISBN 978 0 19 464693 2

The CD has a choice of American and British English
recordings of the complete text.

An accompanying Activity Book is also available,
ISBN 978 0 19 464673 4

Printed in China

This book is printed on paper from certified and
well-managed sources.

ACKNOWLEDGEMENTS

Illustrations by: Kelly Kennedy pp.6, 13; Alan Rowe pp.20, 22,
24, 27, 28, 30, 32, 36, 38, 39.

*The Publishers would also like to thank the following for their kind
permission to reproduce photographs and other copyright material*:
Alamy pp.3 (cows/Inga Spence), 4 (Dennis Frates), 5 (Inga
Spence), 6 (Mira), 7 (rice fields/Jurgen Freund/Bluegreen
Pictures), 8 (tractor/John James), 11 (cows/©Design Pics Inc.
– RM Content), 15 (ostrich farm/Peter Titmuss), 19 (vanilla
plant/Simon Rawles); Corbis pp.3 (banana farm/Christine
Osborne, rice fields/©Sam Diephuis, chickens/Craig Holmes/
Loop Images), 8 (watering crops/Layne Kennedy), 10 (James
L. Amos), 13 (Max Brouwers/Johnér Images), 14 (Craig
Holmes/Loop Images), 17 (David T. Grewcock), 18 (cocoa
farmer/Owen Franken); Getty Images pp.9 (Nigel Pavitt/AWL
Images), 15 (ducks/John Churchman/photolibrary), 16 (net/
Franco Banfi/WaterFrame, feeding fish/Eco Images/Universal
Images Group), 18 (cocoa tree/Bloomberg via Getty Images),
19 (crocodile eggs/photolibrary); Oxford University Press
pp.7 (combine harvester), 11 (milk, cheese, butter, cream
yogurt), 12, 15 (quilt).

In the Mountains

Introduction

Do you eat bread, eggs, fruit, and vegetables? Do you eat meat? Where does this food come from? It comes from farms.

What food grows on farms?
What animals live on farms?
What do farmers do every day?

Now read and discover more about farms!

1 All About Farms

sheep

A Farm

There are many different types of farm. On some farms, there are animals. We get meat, milk, eggs, and wool from animals.

On some farms, there are crops. Crops are plants that we eat or use. We get bread, fruit, and vegetables from crops. On some farms, there are animals and crops.

There are small farms and big farms all around the world. On small farms, there are animals and crops for the farmer's family. On big farms, there are animals and crops for many people.

Farmers work every day. They feed and care for animals, and they plant and grow crops.

A Farmer with Crops

Go to pages 20–21 for activities.

2 Crops

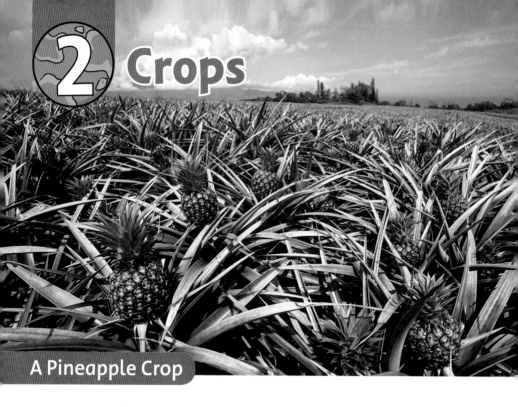

A Pineapple Crop

Crops only grow in the right weather, and with water and good soil.

Bananas and pineapples only grow in hot weather. Strawberries and other soft fruit grow in cool weather.

Discover! A lot of sugar comes from a crop called sugar cane. Sugar cane can grow 9 meters high!

mountain

Rice Terraces

Rice only grows in lots of water. Many farmers grow rice in terraces. Some farmers cut rice terraces into mountains.

Wheat grows in big fields. We make flour from wheat. We use flour to make bread, pasta, and cakes.

A Wheat Crop

→ Go to pages 22–23 for activities.

3 Growing Crops

tractor

plow

Plowing a Field

Some farmers have tractors and lots of big machines to help them to grow crops. Some farmers don't have big machines.

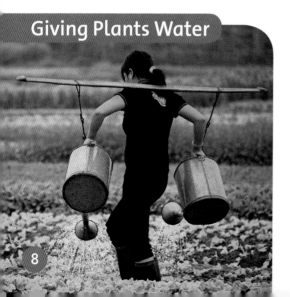

Giving Plants Water

First, farmers plow the fields. Then they plant seeds. The seeds grow into plants. In hot weather, farmers give the plants lots of water.

Some farmers put chemicals on their crops. Chemicals help crops to grow, and they stop animals eating crops. Some farmers grow crops with no chemicals. These are called organic crops.

Later, farmers cut or pick the crops. This is called the harvest.

A Cotton Harvest

cotton flower

Cotton is a crop! Cotton comes from big white flowers on the cotton plant.

Go to pages 24–25 for activities.

4 Cattle

Farmers keep cattle for meat and for milk.

In spring and summer, cattle live in fields and eat lots of grass. In winter, some cattle live in barns. Then they eat dried grass called hay.

Ranches are very big farms. They have lots of fields and lots of cattle. On ranches, farmers use horses to move cattle.

On a Ranch

Farmers milk their cattle every morning and evening. They milk the cattle by hand or with milking machines. We drink the milk. We also make milk into cheese, butter, cream, and yogurt.

milk

butter

yogurt

cheese

cream

Go to pages 26–27 for activities.

5 Sheep

All around the world, there are sheep on farms. We get wool, meat, and milk from sheep.

Sheep can live outside all year. They have a woolen coat called a fleece.

This farmer is shearing a sheep. We use the fleece to make wool. Then we make hats, coats, and socks from the wool.

Shearing

fleece

bottle

Feeding a Lamb

A lamb drinks its mother's milk.
Some sheep can't feed all their
lambs. The farmer feeds these
lambs with milk from a bottle.
Later, lambs eat grass.
Sheep eat grass, too.

To find its mother, a lamb
listens for the noise its
mother makes.

→ Go to pages 28–29 for activities.

6 Poultry

Chickens and other birds on farms are called poultry. We get meat, eggs, and feathers from poultry.

Free-range chickens live outside. Eggs from free-range chickens are very good for you.

On other farms, chickens live in big barns with lots of other chickens. These farms are called factory farms.

Free-Range Chickens

goose duck pillow quilt

Ducks and geese live outside. We use their feathers to make pillows and quilts for our beds.

Some farmers keep ostriches for their eggs, meat, and feathers.

Discover!

An ostrich egg is as big as 40 chicken eggs!

Go to pages 30–31 for activities.

7 Fish

net

There are many different fish farms. Farmers keep fish in lakes, in tanks, or in big nets in the ocean. On fish farms, some fish eat food made from other small fish. Some fish eat plants.

Feeding Fish

lake

16

salmon

Catching Salmon

Farmers feed the fish so they grow big. When fish are big, farmers can sell them. Farmers sell fish fast so they are good to eat.

Lots of salmon come from fish farms. Farmers keep baby salmon in tanks. When the salmon are one year old, farmers put them in nets in the ocean. Farmers catch the salmon and sell them when they are two or three years old.

→ Go to pages 32–33 for activities.

8 Other Farms

We get many different things from farms.

In hot, rainy places, there are lots of cacao farms. Farmers grow cacao trees. They pick the seed pods. They dry the seeds, and then they sell them. People make chocolate with the cacao seeds.

Drying Cacao Seeds

seed pod

cacao tree

seeds

Vanilla Plants

In hot places, farmers grow vanilla plants. We put vanilla in ice cream, cakes, and many other foods.

Some farmers keep crocodiles for their skin and meat. Each crocodile has about 50 eggs. Farmers care for lots of baby crocodiles!

Baby Crocodiles

Around the world, we get our food from farms. We also get many different things that we use every day.

→ Go to pages 34–35 for activities.

1 All About Farms

← Read pages 4–5.

1 Complete the puzzle.

2 Complete the chart.

milk   wool   eggs   vegetables
bread   fruit   meat

From Crops	From Animals	
_____	_milk_	_____
_____	_____	_____
_____		

3 Write *true* or *false*.

1 Crops are plants. _true_

2 We get bread from animals. _____

3 We get meat from animals. _____

4 There aren't any small farms. _____

5 On small farms, there are animals and crops for the farmer's family. _____

6 On big farms, there aren't any animals. _____

4 Match. Then write the sentences.

On some farms	are plants that we eat.
Farmers	comes from animals.
Crops	work every day.
Wool	there are crops.

1 <u>On some farms there are crops.</u>

2 _____

3 _____

4 _____

② Crops

← Read pages 6–7.

1 Write the words.

rice   pineapples
sugar cane   wheat
bananas   strawberries

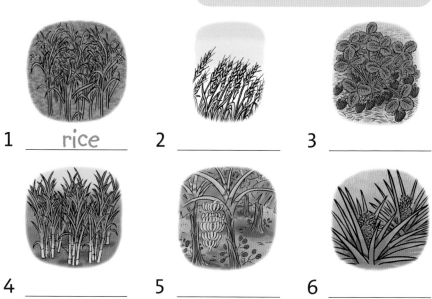

1 ___rice___   2 _____   3 _____

4 _____   5 _____   6 _____

2 Circle the correct words.

1 (Rice)/ **Sugar cane** grows in terraces.

2 We make **flour** / **sugar** from wheat.

3 Sugar cane can grow **nine** / **ninety**
meters high.

4 **Bananas** / **Soft fruits** grow in cool weather.

3 Complete the sentences.

water   soil   cool   ~~weather~~   hot

1 Crops only grow in the right _weather_ ,
   with water and good _____ .

2 Bananas and pineapples grow in
   _____ weather.

3 Strawberries and other soft fruit grow
   in _____ weather.

4 Rice only grows in lots of _____ .

4 Answer the questions.

1 What crop does a lot of sugar come from?
   A lot of sugar comes from a crop
   called sugar cane.

2 Where does wheat grow?
   _____

3 What can you make with flour?
   _____

4 How do farmers make rice terraces in
   mountains?
   _____

23

3 Growing Crops

← Read pages 8–9.

1 Number the sentences in order. Then number the pictures.

☐ Then they plant seeds.

☐ Later, they cut the crops.

☐ | First, farmers plow the fields.

☐ Then they give the plants water.

2 Match.

1 They help farmers.
2 When the farmers cut or pick the crops.
3 It's a crop.
4 Farmers put them on their crops.
5 Farmers grow them with no chemicals.

chemicals
organic crops
cotton
machines
harvest

3 Complete the sentences.

> hot   machines   plants   plow
> organic   seeds

1 Some farmers don't have big _____ .

2 First, farmers _____ the fields.

3 Farmers plant _____ in the fields.

4 Seeds grow into _____ .

5 Farmers give plants lots of water in

  _____ weather.

6 Some farmers grow _____ crops. They
  don't use chemicals.

4 Answer the questions.

1 Do chemicals help crops to grow?

  _____

2 What do chemicals stop?

  _____

3 What are organic crops?

  _____

4 Where does cotton come from?

  _____

4 Cattle

← Read pages 10–11.

1 What do cattle give us? Find and write the words.

a	c	r	e	a	m
c	h	e	e	s	e
m	e	a	t	u	o
a	e	n	u	t	l
l	m	i	l	k	j
b	u	t	t	e	r
y	o	g	u	r	t

1 _cheese_   4 _b_

2 _m_   5 _c_

3 _m_   6 _y_

2 Draw and write about cattle.

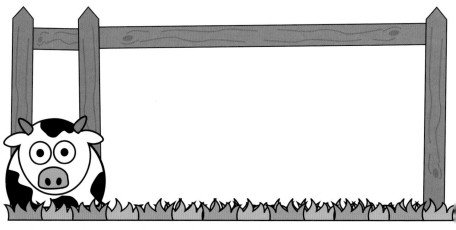

Three things that I know about cattle:

1 _They live in fields in spring and summer._

2 _____

3 _____

3 Complete the sentences. Then write the numbers.

hay   ranch   grass   milk

1 In spring and summer, cattle eat _____ .

2 In winter, some cattle eat _____ .

3 Farmers _____ their cattle every morning and evening.

4 On a _____ , there are lots of fields and lots of cattle.

4 Write *true* or *false*.

1 Some cattle live in barns in winter. _____

2 Ranches are very big farms. _____

3 You can make milk into cheese, butter, cream, and eggs. _____

4 Farmers milk their cattle by hand or with tractors. _____

5 Sheep

← Read pages 12–13.

1 Match. Then write the sentences.

> We use a sheep's
> We use wool
> A lamb

> drinks milk.
> fleece to make wool.
> to make hats.

1 _____

2 _____

3 _____

2 Write the words. Then write the numbers.

1 A baby sheep. (balm)   *lamb*

2 A sheep's coat. (celefe)   _____

3 Lambs eat this. (sasrg)   _____

4 People make this from a
  sheep's fleece. (lowo)   _____

3 Complete the sentences.

> milk   grass   milk   outside
> grass   wool   meat

1 We get _____ , _____ , and
    _____ from sheep.

2 Sheep live _____ all year.

3 Lambs drink _____ . Later, they eat
    _____ .

4 Sheep eat _____ , too.

4 Order the words.

1 meat / sheep. / We / from / get
    _We get meat from sheep._____

2 coat. / Sheep / a / have / woolen
    _____

3 socks / wool. / We / from / make
    _____

4 mother's / drinks / A / lamb / its / milk.
    _____

6 Poultry

← Read pages 14–15.

1 Find and write the words.

featherostrichchickengooseeggsduck

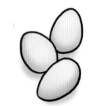

1 _feathers_   2 _____   3 _____

4 _____   5 _____   6 _____

2 Write *F* (factory farms) or *FR* (free-range chickens).

1 Lots of chickens live in big barns.   F

2 The chickens live outside.   _____

3 The eggs are very good for you.   _____

3 Find and write the words.

1 four types of poultry

   geese _____

   _____ _____

2 three things that we get from poultry

   _____ _____ _____

3 two things that we use duck feathers for

   _____ _____

4 three things that we get from ostriches

   _____ _____ _____

4 Answer the questions.

1 What are farm birds called?

   _____

2 Where do ducks and geese live?

   _____

3 What do farmers keep ostriches for?

   _____

4 How big is an ostrich egg?

   _____

7 Fish

← Read pages 16–17.

1 Write the words.

food   lake   net
ocean   fish   tank

1 _____

2 _____

3 _____

4 _____

5 _____

6 _____

2 Circle the correct words.

1 Some farmers keep fish in **food** / **lakes**.

2 Farmers feed fish so they grow **small** / **big**.

3 When fish are big, farmers can **stop** / **sell** them.

4 Farmers sell fish fast so they are **good** / **bad** to eat.

3 Match. Then write the sentences.

Farmers feed fish	come from fish farms.
When fish are big,	so they grow big.
Lots of salmon	farmers can sell them.

1 _____

2 _____

3 _____

4 Complete the sentences.

tanks   nets   fish   sell   lakes   ocean

1 Some farmers keep fish in big _____ in the ocean.

2 Some farmers keep fish in _____ in tanks.

3 Farmers keep baby salmon in _____ .

4 When salmon are one year old, farmers put them in nets in the _____ .

5 When fish grow big, farmers can _____ them.

8 Other Farms

← Read pages 18–19.

1 Write *true* or *false*.

1 Cacao grows in cold, dry places. _____

2 Farmers dry cacao seeds. _____

3 Farmers grow vanilla plants
   in hot places. _____

4 Crocodile farmers keep crocodiles
   for their feathers and meat. _____

5 Each crocodile has about five eggs. _____

2 Complete the sentences.

skin   seeds   trees   vanilla   seed pods

1 Cacao seed pods grow on _____ .

2 Farmers pick the _____ .

3 Then, farmers dry the _____ .

4 We put _____ in ice cream, cakes,
   and other foods.

5 Farmers keep crocodiles for their _____
   and meat.

3 **Where do these things come from?**
Find and write the words.

c	o	t	t	o	n	e	r
t	r	x	o	m	e	a	t
f	e	a	t	h	e	r	s
w	a	b	r	e	a	d	t
w	o	o	l	r	i	c	e
o	s	e	g	g	s	e	t
l	m	i	l	k	s	w	i

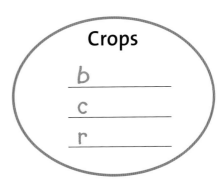

Crops

b _____

c _____

r _____

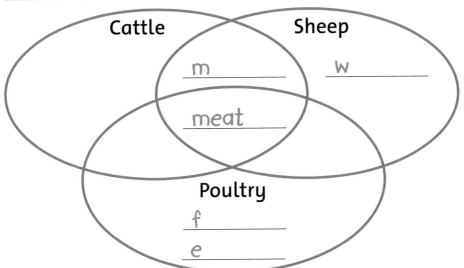

Cattle

Sheep

m _____

w _____

meat

Poultry

f _____

e _____

4 **Where do these things come from? Match.**

1 chocolate   birds

2 butter   wheat

3 bread   cacao

4 feathers   milk

My Farm

1 Think of a farm. Draw and label the things on your farm. Then write about it.

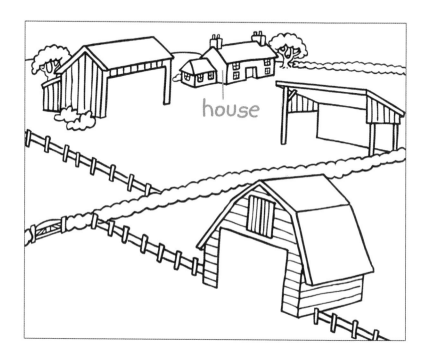

house

My farm is called: _____

I grow these crops: _____

_____

I keep these animals:

_____

Animals on Farms

1 Write about animals on farms.

Name: _cattle_

Eat: _grass and hay_

Live: _in fields and barns_

We get: _meat and milk_

Name: _____

Eat: _____

Live: _____

We get: _____

Name: _____

Eat: _____

Live: _____

We get: _____

Picture Dictionary

 barn

 chemicals

 coat

 cool

 cotton

 crops

 cut

 farm

 fast

 feathers

 fields

 flour

 food

 fruit

 grass

 grow

hay

machine

meat

pick

plant

plants

sell

skin

soil

strawberries

seeds

sugar

tank

vegetables

wool

world

Oxford Read and Discover

Series Editor: Hazel Geatches • CLIL Adviser: John Clegg

Oxford Read and Discover graded readers are at six levels, for students from age 6 and older. They cover many topics within three subject areas, and support English across the curriculum, or Content and Language Integrated Learning (CLIL).

Available for each reader:
• Audio CD Pack (book & audio CD)
• Activity Book

Teaching notes & CLIL guidance: www.oup.com/elt/teacher/readanddiscover

Subject Area / Level	The World of Science & Technology	The Natural World	The World of Arts & Social Studies
1 300 headwords	• Eyes • Fruit • Trees • Wheels	• At the Beach • Camouflage • In the Sky • Young Animals	• Art • Schools
2 450 headwords	• Electricity • Plastic • Sunny and Rainy • Your Body	• Earth • Farms • In the Mountains • Wild Cats	• Cities • Jobs
3 600 headwords	• How We Make Products • Sound and Music • Super Structures • Your Five Senses	• Amazing Minibeasts • Animals in the Air • Life in Rainforests • Wonderful Water	• Festivals Around the World • Free Time Around the World
4 750 headwords	• All About Plants • How to Stay Healthy • Machines Then and Now • Why We Recycle	• All About Desert Life • All About Ocean Life • Animals at Night • Incredible Earth	• Animals in Art • Wonders of the Past
5 900 headwords	• Materials to Products • Medicine Then and Now • Transportation Then and Now • Wild Weather	• All About Islands • Animal Life Cycles • Exploring Our World • Great Migrations	• Homes Around the World • Our World in Art
6 1,500 headwords	• Cells and Microbes • Clothes Then and Now • Incredible Energy • Your Amazing Body	• All About Space • Caring for Our Planet • Earth Then and Now • Wonderful Ecosystems	• Food Around the World • Helping Around the World

Readers in GRAY available 2013